Food Clothes & Shelter

Sugar Johnson

ISBN:0692624899
ISBN-13: 9780692624890

To my mother, Maizey P. Serrette, only Heaven has the words that describe my love and appreciation for you.

CONTENTS

FOREWORD

Why Food Clothes and Shelter?

Because some young ambitious history makers named Bobby and Huey stood up to rep "it" as the highest aspiration of Black people to this date, this simple triumvirate, food, clothes and shelter stands at the center of today's primary contradiction. War, Poverty, Sexism and even Tupac's murderer are secondary contractions connected to the web that stands between us and happiness. Like Frankie Beverly would say, "That's the golden time of day!" We all look forward to it. And when I met this brother named Sugar Johnson, I knew he was too in search of that Happiness on the Other Side. Within only a few meetings it was clear to me that he does what the great ones do...soak up our environment and reflect it upon us in such a nourishing way. We have much work to do, let him help you do yours. WON!!!

- M1

SUGAR JOHNSON

PLANTATION HYMNALS

"Lord it's so hard living this life, a constant struggle each and every day. Some wonder why I'd rather die than to continue living this way." – Goodie Mob

40 Years, No Acres and I'm the Mule

it's the tale of inferiors and superiors

deadlines

spreadsheets

and well-articulated phone greetings

the sound of footsteps sashaying to the next meeting

ass kissers invading personal space

lunch time

one hour

set your watch

your being watched

monitored

praying for vacation time

or just some time to clean the basement

plant some tomatoes

take a long shower

pushing for that raise

hell even a promotion

politics

politricks

gotta do better than that

'cause Molly licks

tapered haircuts

and starched shirts

cuffed trousers

401K contributions

allocation

and health insurance needs

invest in your future

make money til your back hurts

or you're fed up with your commute

whichever comes first

40 years

10400 days

minus Christmas and Thanksgiving

dreams spread thin

like the cobwebs

stuck to the guitar

I always told myself I'd learn to play

Like Water for Massa

swallowing essential liquid

soothing mind and throat

soften desire for pacification

ease physiological fire alarm

approach equilibrium

enter necessary sales data

smooth numbers for VP and Director

comfort mind of Manager

fend off desk seeking nuisance

4:58 on Friday

A Small Promotion

He was nothing like they think of us

his eyes squinting

from the large smile that adorned his face

talking to an old friend

about his promotion

from flyer distributing foot soldier

to bike operating pizza guy

his voice wrapped in excitement

as he talked about doing something better

he was happy to be working

happy to be feeding his family

happy to be sharing the news

Just for Today

just for today

i'll acknowledge the sound of the alarm clock

coordinate business casual attire

to fit the bill

pass the old men

halfway wishing I could join them on the crates by the
liquor store

rush to a train i really wanna miss

just for today

i'll say good morning

when i'd rather not speak

absorb insensitive "I didn't mean anything by it"
comments

smile

instead of cuss

or cry

or crack every bone that matters

just for today

i'll move out of your way

though you act like you can't see me

help you

let them think you're smart

when you're not

just for today

i'll listen to my brother

find every reason

to blame everyone but himself

watch his wife

smooth things out

with no appreciation

cringe

as my sister acts like a bitch

under the guise of pleasing my mother

just for today

i'll complain about things

instead of work to fix them

or rather myself

hide between realities

thinking it's safe

on the bridge connecting this world and the next

just for today

cuz tomorrow will be different

i'll be different

just for today

Corporate Success

they rarely come to the city

you could tell

ostrich boots for the rain

a simple gold band

miniature umbrella

five dollar magazine

perfectly creased pants

with the hanger wrinkle in the middle

America's success story

they married out of college

in Iowa

made a life here in NY

he works on Wall Street

she followed him here to teach 3rd grade

her family's wealthy

that's how they got the house

he's now the VP of the Mutual Fund Group

in the corner office on the 43rd floor

with the perfect view

of the building across the street and a spot of the Hudson

he played basketball in college

cuz his dad did

but his dream

is the fast talking

fast walking

fast track

for him

it's like acting in a feature film

where the plot is your life

praying every night

the good guy gets the girl

and the gold

so here they are

with me

on the 3 train

probably on their way to a Broadway show

to watch someone else's dream unfold

he's so excited

that she's excited

he can't even sit down

The Bell Tolls

I'm being pushed and shoved into sobriety

after a quick morning shower

staggering down the concrete stairs

to the beat of grumpy thoughts

surrounded by people

that refuse to deem me visible

not even for an excuse me

one part of the mind daydreaming

of financial freedom

and road trips

and tours

and having people over to watch the fight

the other part

labouring for intellectual fulfillment

with Achebe

and James

and Patton

and Benjamin

trying to fit in as much understanding

as the transport time will allow

but I've arrived at the place

where I begin my secular day

I hesitate

cuz I wanna stay seated

and see what the Bronx looks like

from the elevated train tracks

I wanna sit on my stoop

and see what the old men talk about

before they get drunk

I wanna be some place

with no place to go

but I gotta work

the bell tolls

and I'm gonna miss my stop

LATE

NIGHT

KITCHEN

FOLK

TALES

"Good food ends with good talk" – Geoffrey Neighor

What the Pot Said to the Spoon

one flew over the coo coo's nest

cuz love don't make no sense

lest you know

that ain't the last one to fly over the fence

hard back mermaids shakin' tail feathers

got us not knowin' whether to shit or go blind

drive us to drink

like we got a hollow leg

rubber necks test elasticity

to how she can strut you into a stupor

don't act like you ain't got good sense

pockets ain't got more than lint and bubble gum

fresh outta gum

trying to buy time

slow dancin' with the wind

til she spills the beans

she says

too many cooks will spoil the soup

'specially if it's bitches brew

go hard

or go home

it's the chase they're after

pump your brakes

smell the roses

see which one you like

can't put all your eggs in one basket case

gold

ain't the only thing glittering

she'll come

when you're done worrying about the weather

enjoy the view

just don't lose your head

over a lil piece of tail

Queen Elizabeth

it was the mmm hmmm after a profound statement

assuring me she was telling the truth

eyes blessed with recording volumes of down home
happenings

ear drums danced a knee slapping vibrato

to the B flat concerto

of a simple walk down the street

she knew all the parables Jesus didn't tell the masses

held true to a creed before the invention of books and
glasses

though she had a pair

cuz her medicine had small letters on the label

laughed from the depths of her pepper steak filled
stomach

with the sincerity of a love letter's salutation

cared for me like she taught me to tie my shoes

Gramma Lowe

living proof that blood don't mean a damn thing

and water is for drinking

Us

we're all human

black

red

brown

and blue in the face

from trying to explain our truth

fragile and strong

singing our favorite song

wishing we could do what we wanted

all day long

criminal and mischievous

evil and sadistic

slappin booties

cuz we love the sound

kissing lips

cuz we love the taste

slow and smooth

like a neat cognac

wild and crazy

like Ash Wednesday Eve

Eastern Parkway to Four Roads

Manchester to Johannesburg

we're all human

Fifty Years Later

It was like the first time he put hammer to nail

seeing her slide across the room

Maybe it was the soft pleats

or the jet black high heel shoes

all he knew was that Pat Boone

and Bill Haley were on the radio,

the Honeymooners were on TV

and Rudolph Flesch was ranting

about Johnny not being able to read

Roy Campanella was playing for the Dodgers

Roy Rogers was more than a restaurant

and James Dean was wearing blue jeans

and driving fast cars

I think it was the way she made him smile

like a young boy on Christmas morning

she was the perfect woman

born with the ability to transform thread and cloth

into the latest fashion

and she could turn scraps

into a warm satisfying meal

Love wasn't the question,

it's the answer

Arts,

crafts

and cooking

were a vehicle to bringing the family together

and boy are they together

Fifty years later

Pat Boone isn't on the radio

and everyone is wearing jeans,

but Nat King Cole is still Unforgettable,

she's still the perfect woman

and he's still smiling like it's Christmas

A Woman's Support

(To Dun)

It was the greatest barbecue sauce

you ever tasted in your natural life

folks would smother their baked chicken with that sauce

his father was so proud of his tableside concoction

the family enjoyed on their home cooked Sunday evening meal

he always had his wife taste it before it was served

so that it was certified the best damn sauce ever made

to his amazement

she agreed night after night

ensuring her husband remained the household's man

and as his poked out chest made its way to the dining room

she topped the sauce with a woman's savor

adding everything it needed

to be as superb as people expected

his father had no idea

and love always lived in the kitchen

Mama's Pie

(inspired by Satin Bell – P. S. 27)

Two teaspoons of gospel

a dash of rock

2 cups of jazz

1 cup of hip hop (use rap for substitute)

3 cups of crazy

stir contents

mix with apples, pears, bananas and mango

add an ounce of calypso and reggae

half a cup of salsa (preferably mambo)

add a little water and melted sugar

mix thoroughly

pour into honey crust

heat oven to 333 degrees

bake

check in 7 minute intervals until brown

let it cool

and serve the community

Order of Our Lady of Green Funk

A society with secrets

some of which only the street dwellers dare to understand

the handshake resides in the fellowship

hand to Earth

finger to finger

slide finger

you've seen it before

right in your homeboy's living room

we have no meeting place

save the family rooms of the land

family is who we are

finger pricking came through us

we've since moved on

to picking apart the breaths of air

alive in the multicolored arrangements

to Jah and Shango

blue isn't the only color of jazz

descendants of the world's indigenous people

we are the Loo Loo

kissing our food before we taste it

relishing in the rituals of meal preparation

seeing the world as it is

a mountainous community of ideas

love and elevation our creed

the green leaf our emblem

our motto

is to use the Earth wisely

and responsibly

take a deep breath

sit back

and revere nature

Do you um?

SUGAR JOHNSON

Tale of Two Cities

The first lesson of martial arts is

not to use it

parents telling you not to do things they've done

and liked

hard work pays off

while hardly working

pays better

listen carefully

speak your mind

be sensitive

but don't take no shit

it's all a paradox

our very existence

is like the tale of two cities

ethereal beings

in earthly space suits

trying to make choices

that have already been predestined

organizing time

that is not our own

reading new books

to remind ourselves

of what we already knew

looking for love

outside of where it should reside

inside

what you learn to do is

control what you can

and marvel at the rest

record what you learn

and pass it on

no time to worry about extras

you're here to enjoy yourself

just be careful

the paradox

HOLLA

IF

YOU

HEAR

ME

"If you see everybody dying because of what you saying, it doesn't matter that you didn't make them die, it just matters that you didn't save them." – Tupac Shakur

Fuck Jesse

Mr. Cool Man

Mr. Starched Shirt Man

the white man's number one fan

' cause they puttin money in your hand

makin' you believe you doin' all you can

Mr. Wanna be President

but the race ran away like the Ginger Bread Man

too busy fuckin' with them hoes man

lisa denise debra and jan

Mookie you gotta take care of your kids man

makin comments on movies

and like Smokey said,

"You didn't put in on this man!"

hope your punk ass ain't workin' for the Klan

'cause you're selective when you wanna give a damn

need to listen to "What Would You Say" by the Dave
Matthews Band

I say

FUCK JESSE

tell his ass I said to work on being a family man.

Spoken Word

books are sacred

oral tradition just as important

some stories were never transcribed

listening and writing is difficult

other times

fear and suppression stifled sound record keeping

like in 1796

slaves whispering late night renditions of breeding
practices

women worth more if sex was profitable

strong men valued by the use of their genetic code

a machine in a machine

these days ain't no different

young mothers sponsored by the government

on high rise plantations

birth young thugs

to increase funding for any upstate you can think of

from Terre Haute to Rikers Isle

cheap labor forces

housed in institutions

built commensurate to urban reading scores

funding rural communities

based on a captive population

unwritten tragedies

that would make even Shakespeare cry

hate crimes discussed in dark corners

cuz master can't take real truth

talking about third eyes is cool

but what good is a third eye

if you're not using the others

to see that history repeats itself

How Many Times

How many times can you talk about riding with the
shooting spear

cocked for your enemies

how many times can you dress women in skimpy clothes

as they play the background role to the newest song

that don't mean shit

how many times can you try to make us believe

the pursuit of shiny things

can replace real relationships

and living like we got sense

how many times can you pub high price designers

that cringe when you walk into their stores

how many times can you forget the purpose of your gift
for words

how many times can you buy tricks with wheels

instead of sending a young fan off to college

to learn more about themselves

how many times can you think telling the same story will

elevate us

ok so she liked your car

and you got some

and she won't stop paging you cuz you gotta ride or die for
your niggas

and the bitch in the crew that you're fuckin' too

so big deal

I'm doing that shit

and I ain't even got no car

so we ride or die on the train

but how many times

how many times

you gon say the same stupid shit

and call it art

Just Say the Shit

I'm tired of poems

that sound like you are talking

to some sort of beat in your head.

You don't have to change cadence in your voice

to exemplify what you said.

With that kinda poetry

you can read a phone book

and be profound.

When the truth is,

folks are just mesmerized

by the change in sound.

I blame Darius Lovehall

for making cats believe poetry

is all about incense and augmented jazz chords,

but real poetry is seen

when there's no lights and no stage

and someone is writing with all their heart can afford.

I get on the mic cuz I'm kinda fucked up

and talking to you helps me through my day.

Cuz best believe if what I write ain't popular

I'm readin' it anyway.

So tell me 'bout the skin I'm in

when you decide to put that black to white.

The truth is a lot of folks can act

but very few can write.

A Sugar Coat and a Band Aid

striking deals with the devil

having demons teach the kids

don't pray to your God

worship clothes and cash

giving up ass to pass

and still can't read

guns not solving problems

or equations

no sense of human relation

paving the road to destruction

thwarted history mistaken for instruction

little concern for trouble kids

more about securing the highest bid

corporate sponsorship the goal

but the books are still old

grumpy teachers caught up in times past

while students' lives go by real fast

these days school is more like punishment

no recess, music or mental nourishment

security getting more funding

meanwhile curriculum's redundant

ill-prepared for anti-urban standardized tests

they fail, drop out you know the rest

from Kings County all the way to Tilden

it's all about control

cuz it damn sure ain't about the children

Where Will You Be?

where will you be in May?

when the New World Order starts

when they take away the subway token

and force feed you the Metrocard

where will you be?

when they get rid of the US dollar

and replace it with New Dollars

when they can run up in your crib

without a warrant

and it's constitutional

where will you be?

when you find out that dumb president

ain't really that dumb

when he's affecting policy

that allow us to walk the street

without being questioned

where will you be?

when your homeboy with the 'dro hookup

is sent to a concentration camp in Guantanamo Bay

when your favorite football player's name

is Mr. Roboto

when cabs really stop going to the hood

because the address is not in the GPS system

where will you be?

when you hear that funny click and the sound of open
space

during every phone conversation

when you stop needing a change of address form

to have your bills sent to the new crib

where will you be?

when the underground movement

is really underground

and you have to give Harriet's great great great great great
great-granddaughter

the password

where will you be?

when American Express Blue

is the proud sponsor of the chips

they put in your kids

you know the animals already have 'em

the real question is

where will you be

mentally,

spiritually?

where will you be?

Pass It Down

they done raised the price of oatmeal cookies

from 25 cents to 40 cents

the Dow Jones is at an all-time slant

S&P is sniffing and puffing on the backs of hardworking Americans

or shall I say US citizens

we know all the specifications of the latest automobiles

made from materials of oppression

and an imperialistic mind frame

we've mastered selling fake dreams

using the tube and speaker as the oracle

all while forgetting Sunday dinner at Aunt KiKi's

were the times we knew ourselves

when music and fellowship kept even the most dysfunctional families together

all in all we survived the cold weather

let's not forget what really keeps us alive

so go look in the mirror

tell that motherfucker in front of you

you love them

and pass it down

A Black Man with a Muslim Name

So they found him,

the sniper.

Thirteen people shot,

3 survivors.

Our kids weren't safe,

400 yards away,

one shot killin' ya,

a Fort Lewis certified gunman.

They found him,

a Black man with a Muslim name.

That makes sense,

a person of color

with an Al Qaeda connection

through his surname.

I guess H. Rap Brown will have a cell mate.

Next thing you know

they'll be arresting Cassius Clay

for droppin' too many white boys

after he changed his name.

They found him

with a young boy

talking about the most talked about subject in past weeks.

So what we can't talk about crime the cops can't prevent anymore?

Or did Congress sign that right over too?

I mean what in the world

would a Black man have to gain

from killing ten people

with a high powered rifle.

We just trying to survive.

We ain't got time for that shit!

A Message from the Crazy House

Pops left the crib

and mom with baby in hand.

Brown eyes

blurry with tears

wondering what to do;

no hope,

no escape

and no money to change the locks.

WIC applications take too long,

McDonald's can't feed the family

and the corner store ain't giving out no more food on credit.

Her 7-pound infant wearing recycled pampers

and oversized t-shirts to keep warm.

So confused

she ran away from reality,

from life,

too many questions,

no time for answers,

no time to think,

no means,

no ends,

odd job trading for potato chip dinners.

So she bartered her son for mobility –

a child could really slow you down.

The baby changes hands,

homes,

and identity.

A new life,

another chance,

clean clothes,

and fresh towels.

Programmed for success,

trained to love,

groomed for survival

and all I have to say is...

I'm not sorry.

JUST

SOME

SHIT

I

WROTE

"No quote needed." – Alvin W.

Just Some Shit I Wrote

I was born on Cool Mu'fucka Street

between Integrity Lane and Honesty Place

and it's a gated community

Untitled #119

loud screams

sighs

traveling wireless conduits

generate enough heat for a frustrated stew

with a dash of shame

disdain

hearts pump speedily

for fear of paradoxical freedom

soft eye lids hold back early morning showers

clear skies will take a while

reality took a big bite of her love sandwich

and drank the last of the Kool Aid

Interestingly Untitled

Aquarian foreheads pointing towards the heavens

Saturn influencing low tolerance for bullshit

Jupiter's moons busied with getting things done

we are all children of a diverse planetary distribution

clocking in on Earth cuz we have work to do

chasing dreams aligned with our duty

only to go on vacation

leaving our essence behind

returning to respective leisure homes

waiting for the next assignment

playing in sonic fields with our galactic cousins

riding comets

taking naps on the moon

'til Gramma calls us inside

we got House work to do

there's an opening for a World Changer

back to Earth

wave goodbye to Parent Planet

duty always callin'

maybe this time I'll accumulate more vacation time

put a little more in the retirement fund

Mercurial Atmosphere

One person

divided into two

multiplied by enough red blood cells

to go around the world 2.3 times

the mathematical composition

of what evolves into two separate parts

conjoined via astral connection

the integral of a private language

understanding beyond our ability to dream of green
pastures

moving as one person

dually present

like a sneeze in the kitchen

and a bless you from the bedroom

living to change the world

with only solid trust in each other

no one else

not even mother

the life of a twin

Untitled #227

there's a little pet shop

on the east side of the city

they have all kinds of sea animals and stuff

in the window there's this massive tank

with fish you don't see on the reg

and this gourmet food delivery guy standing in front of it

mentally reallocating his funds

to adjust

for having that very tank in his living room

you can tell he stops there everyday

between deliveries

daydreaming

just like my experience at the music store

looking up and down the aisles

wishing I had to squeeze past the Monk and Montgomery

to get to my kitchen

two people

hoping one day

the 9 to 5

will pay for the six to eight.

URBAN

HAIKU

"Take your words and scrape the sky, shake rain on the desert." – Etheridge Knight

Domestic Violence

I fall asleep to

the faucet giving the sink

cold Chinese torture.

Collard Greens

Like chocolate cake

no nutritional value

a guilty pleasure

To the Point

Make her smile and laugh

Enjoy ev'ry moment spent

So she takes clothes off

Fried Fish Thoughts

Nobody knows where I'm from

I do

I just can't tell myself yet

Bling Ding

So if you fell in love with my chain

What happens when I take it off

Will you marry the dresser?

All Dogs Go To Heaven

I think good people

come back as dogs

with rich caretakers

Miracle Whip or Hellman's

Make good sweet lovin'

Preparing turkey sandwich

Asked crucial question

Stop Whining

Struggle is human

Yours ain't no worse than mine

Especially when you're my boss

The Highest Praise

I think Hallelujah

is Thank You

in the language of the angels

LONGING

"Thrill me out of my senses. Save me. Take me. Hurt me. But make me love you. Make me your slave." – Robert Beck

Sweet Honey

I'm afraid

I won't meet her before I close my eyes

or hold her hand

down a normal street

after dinner

at the best hole in the wall spot

that I won't know what her fingers feel like in my beard

or how deeply she breathes while asleep

I'm afraid

I'll never have to buy a baby chair

a baby seat

a toy for teething

I'm afraid

she won't be there

as my feet traverse foreign soil

distant beaches

Egyptian sand

I'm afraid

she'll stay in my dreams

cuz it's safe there

she has all my attention

I'm afraid

that I know her already

and she's afraid of me

cuz I'm just that strange

but she'll come

when I'm ready for her

to be ready for me

Yet Untitled But Sexy

It's the all-time greatest physical feeling in the world

the only split second your spirit, soul, heart, and mind

dine at the same table

she opens her portal to a world you can never understand

until you've lived there for a minute

and I don't mean sixty seconds

one of the only places where the longer you stay

the longer you're welcome

a secret city where you have to know the password

and be a SCUBA diver of the highest regard

immersing yourself in a sea of living waters

with perfect temperature

it's like laying under a soft sky blue comforter

with the A/C on medium

a semi-strong breeze

after a great workout

holding her closer

than your third layer of skin

spoon feeding her lobes

with words that make her goose bumps

look like the pimples of our adolescence

enter her private room

learning how deep the rabbit hole goes

she gasps

and you find out the exact location of Eden

the position of the Earth when the moon is in retrograde

the precise measurement of pi

the reason Orion made it to the heavens

and how Gramma makes stew chicken fall off the bone

it's where we always wanna go

baby will you take me there...

again

Be Goroyanigering (Tell Me In My Ear)

She's beautiful in every way

And I can't describe the way she looks

because her eyes perceive my thoughts and feelings

my premonitions and fears

when she looks at me

I imagine caramel legs

wrapped around my waist

her lips pressed against my neck

whispering how she wants her wine to flow like waterfalls

she wants me not to think about her

but make love as free flowing as her hair –

that forest covering a mind

imagining my lotioned hands caressing her inner thighs,

summoning her throbbing love mechanism

She's beautiful in every way…

I can't help but think about her soft peppermint voice

kissing my heart

easing the pain of daily cultural judo matches

her hands resting on a stomach

filled with the satisfaction that she's near me

telling me her eardrum beats to the rhythm of a song

sang only to the entity

with skin

warmed by Ethiopian sun.

She's beautiful in every way…

The heartbeat that pounds on a chest

wet with the imprint of her lips

lips that dispose of my evil thoughts

reminding me that my mind is filled with greatness

and will one day be the channel through which creativity
flows

where making undying sound inwardly concentrated

becomes the tune to which she will capture my heart

with the net of compassion

and free me

from the hook of confusion.

She is beautiful in every way…

You Gotta Tell 'Em They're Beautiful

Something about young female athletes

makes you wonder what they do when they're not playing

for me it was the way she hit the ball

making shots you couldn't teach

cat like grace

and power you swore was a release for domestic
frustration

a young thang

wondering why I concerned myself with her scholastic
endeavors

and choice of tunes

telling her she was beautiful

brought on the same reaction

a stink bum gets for soliciting loose change

she dug the pretty boy type

cats who bust nuts

and never bothered to ask about feelings

fucking it up for the next five people

he just wanted their sexual encounters

to be

on tomorrow's Crown Heights Gazette

I wanted her to set high goals

but I didn't care

cuz you gotta tell 'em

you gotta tell young girls they're beautiful.

Public School Pipe Dreams

Her name ended with an "isha"

like most girls at that time

my little pee pee would get hard

imagining what my fourth grade mind

could sum up as to what sex was

her stomach was my turn-on

I knew nothing of fat booties

or wet coochies

she was of East Indian descent

her distinct features

snatched every penny of attention I could afford

I shoulda known then

that normalcy was not my companion

instead irregularity would be my side arm

she had large protruding ears

and jet black satin hair

the infallible motion of her slender frame

turned the streets of Crown Heights

into London runways

She was better than R&B...

ahhh

my fourth grade fantasy

The One Thing I Didn't Expect

I left feeling pretty good that evening

wind saturated with spells of pneumonia

I couldn't feel a thing

I had had the perfect night

and there was nothing anyone could tell me

that would change my mind

I've had this feeling before

but tonight was somehow different

she was wearing black pants

and a soft cotton top

with an open back

our eyes met during one of my favorite songs

I noticed her instructing her friend

in watching me act a fool on the dance floor

I smiled

an inadvertent thanks for her approval

as my dance partner in the near future

I decided to ask her a simple question

not because I wanted to know the obvious answer

but to reciprocate the interest

I thought she was trying to privy me to earlier in the night

well we danced

as the heat

began to take over hairdos and steam pressed clothes

our attention was fixed on each other

body movements

exchanging smiles

hip touches

gestures of delight

her cool demeanor

warded off the staring eyes

of envious onlookers

even they noticed the uniqueness

of the situation

as we contorted our bodies in pure contentment

of the DJ's vinyl crowd pleasers

I didn't bother to follow instructions

from the handbook entitled *Getting Her Number at the Club*

the moments were beautiful

getting her name didn't cross my mind once

like I said it was perfect

that night her name was Thank You

and mine…

You're Welcome.

A Black Woman Named Peggy

making punch

in a kitchen

that reminded me of movies I watched after Sunday dinner

wearing a sexy-but-I'll-tell-you-how-it-is dress

no shoes

revealing feet

you were sure walked the planks

of an 1850s Southern Baptist Church

a vintage soul

she greeted you in a way

that urged you to take off your hat

and address her as ma'am

she could tell stories

like the trees between Florida and Georgia

a black woman named Peggy

serving fresh fried fish cakes

where the secret ingredient

was the love housed in her fingers

moving like a breeze

between the living room and front door

present but unseen

possessing the spirit of a woman

that visits me

between the ascension of the moon

and my morning walk to the train

the woman of my dreams

told me how to reach her during the day

doesn't mean we'll be together

I just feel blessed to have seen her dance

Gratuity

She had 2 kids

i still wanted to be in her presence

she handed me my vanilla shake

i was dying to slurp her softness instead

did everything right

so i asked for the number

hoping for the opportunity

to be a repeat offender

in her subway of addictive flesh

she owned the cutest little butt

one that wouldn't take control

of the space in the bed

i wanted to encapsulate her

with what i knew she was missing,

or rather

what I hoped she would fiend for in my absence

But timing

seemingly disturbing phone calls

and those two cute kids

never allowed enough time…

time to know how soft her skin really was

Jasmine

It was bliss

the soft tingling of the lipstick on your lips

as they reflected the scattered light in such a dark room.

Your smile stood at the forefront of the shadows

lurking behind the poles

that separated me from your touch.

The lint in my pocket

weighed me down in the seat

as my mind pondered what nickname you possessed.

The air overflowing with hard dicks,

hopes

and dreams of a better life

was dampened by the vapor of loneliness,

hard times

and a lack of gas money.

I, too,

lusted after the services this place presented

despite the notion of sin

and what people would think of me tomorrow.

It was the exchange of hot breath

and conversational kisses

that allowed for our enjoyment of being in the same place.

Your heart was padlocked

and emotions wore thin

as bulged eyes imagined reality

coupled with the messages your body was sending.

I was mesmerized

by the cloud-like texture of your soft hello.

The more words we exchanged

the more my soul wished to be embraced by your own.

Your soft scent

satisfied my hunger for affection,

your movement

as soothing as a massage.

Help me not get used to this

or think that reality functions in accordance with the rules
of the world

behind these doors.

Your light caramel skin

was an added plus

to the pleasure that lie in each strand of your dark hair.

I was in love

with the moment

and the imprint it left on my dreams as I lay to rest.

Money can't buy what I experienced that night,

but it'll do...

for now.

What I Pay For

I pay money

to get stuffed into a room

where the body heat alone

could melt the polar ice caps

watching women dance to songs

that leave nothing to the imagination

men scavenging for pretty eyes

long hair

and voluptuous body parts

or someone who just wants to dance

I pay money to float off into space

to the thumpin' bass

trying not to stare at women

caught up in fashionable jewelry

and the latest gadgets

'cause the truth is

I just don't have A plus credit

and no desire to be fashionably loud

I always wonder why I come here

What do I hope to gain or accomplish?

Am I really having a good time?

Or just pretending to be enjoying that song?

I guess maybe

my hope is that I

can turn an unfamiliar booty

into a familiar heartbeat

close to mine

at the dawn of a new day.

Cognitive Shift

Tired of writing the poem through the glass

window shopping on life

talking about how I saw her from a distance

wishing we could converse

instead

I've chosen to write about the time

we sat next to each other on the train

when I politely asked her name

heard frustration in her voice

between the lines of where she worked

and where she wanted to be

which looked something like home

gave her my card

explaining how we could go anywhere her right brain
could conceive

and my left could achieve

saying that calling me would be a good start

so she did

we met for dinner

made love

between the collard greens

and pillow talk

like seeing tomorrow was a long shot

this happened

it's beautiful

try it

Serious

why so serious my love

why dost thine eyes fail to meet mine

as we pass on the road

hast our kind hurt thee so

shant we exchange pleasantries

that make the day brighter

why so serious my love

dost the wind not penetrate the strands of your hair

wash them in natural affection

has compassion forgotten your name

fear become your confidante

why so serious my love

dost not my need for acquaintance

not match your own

does ignoring me ease the pain

of past relations

why so serious my love

paint a smile on thy face

and complete a masterpiece

Lisa

As I journey in the darkness

beyond the stop sign

I ponder silence's golden value

and the platinum-like worth of her subject

when I opened the door

after washing my hands of love's semiconductor

no music satisfied the soft rim of my eardrum

like your candied breath

whispering wonderful wants

there is no hard evidence of your presence

but my tingling hands tell me I touched you

and the imprints on the couch

tell me you were here

Need A Change

Lick

suck

touch

feel

grab

pull

grunt

stick

bend

bow

flip

slap

slap

slap

kiss

lick

squeeze

touch

feel

breathe

gasp

sigh

whimper

touch

tap

smile

giggle

call me Thursday

yeah

all that shit is cool

rather have someone

for my Sunday afternoons

Untitled #145

had me giddy

like wearing your favorite outfit to school

on Friday

working hard throughout the day

knowing relaxing with her

was worth a full day of class

two jobs

and a 2 hour conference call

understood me like an obedient canine

insecurities traded for long hugs

and affectionate pillow talk

my in house counselor

constantly making plans

to meet me on the other side

of closed eye lids

I always wonder

if I will ever love like that again

maybe

I don't think

I can be that vulnerable

cuz that's what it takes

The Glue

She still puts on that Ponds cream before church

does her hair with a hot comb

whipping up meals wrought by Caribbean upbringing

filling me up for hours

she still believes in bathing

even when in the shower

the fusion of Ivory soap

and her pH balance

are a natural summertime bug repellent

made cleaning the yard at 75 a cinch

laughing helps her to remember everything

but her arthritis

she gave up trying to change people

and leans on the everlasting arms

my mother

the most understanding person I know

mastered the art of using a good sandwich

to find out what she needs to know

I think her and Love are sisters

separated at birth

TIES

THAT

BIND

"Family is the undeniable genealogical truth dispersed into the air of difference and slight conflict, melded with sound upbringing, wrapped in the ineffable." – Gus Mayweather

My Wisdom

from afar

you burn the incense of intercession

your voice calms the sea of confusion

helps me weather the storm on my journey

your silver hair full of folk tales

illustrations of your golden experiences

and the struggles that have made you strong

I salute you

mother of my accomplishments

foundation to my mansion of strength

I pray my life is a reflection of your love

and a monument to the courage you have willed me

I love you

Uncle Rust

You are our safe haven

when Momma is working late.

You helped save us from ourselves.

'Cause somehow you knew

that all roads don't lead to the Brooklyn Bridge.

Some of 'em go upstate

and others

six feet underground.

You made being intelligent cool

and challenged our idea of fear.

If our feet hurt

we could always walk on our hands

as long as we get there.

Actually you'd rather we use our hands

as well as our heads

and our hearts.

We wished all our dads were this cool –

those of us who even met our dad.

Sound advice was always what we needed to hear

even if it wasn't what we wanted to hear.

Tuesdays and Thursdays would never be the same.

I still can't hear house music

without thinking about pointing my toes.

It's amazing

how someone with a name like Rusty

could shine so bright.

Although we may not say it out loud,

we love our Uncle Rust.

The Side Effects of Favoritism

hated him for what he did

speaking to him only because he's my brother

his wife

like my mother

begged me not to shut him out

seeing the good in people

went down the drain

like the bullshit used as rationale

for why he hit me

like a stranger

in that mall parking lot

mere hours

after congratulating me on living happily for 18 years

this same day

my nephew

his son

began to pick at my peace

like a scab from a playground accident

my tolerance for childish taunts had since shortened

he persisted

anger had now superseded logic

and cool

so I hit him

repeatedly

I hit him

for the times I was shunned to please him

I hit him

for the times I was beaten because he cried

I hit him

for every time he got his way

but nothing had changed

his father came to save the day

like the Mighty Mouse theme

was somehow playing in his head

his son

was in trouble

he needed to be saved from his evil uncle

reminding me of the many times he was saved

from facing what he deserved

tears began to flow in a way that blurred my vision

laying backwards over a rail

having a serious conversation with the ceiling

about this being the last time I'd be seen in this position

or be seen at all

carried the pain on my sleeve

uncertain of love's power

family has a way

of helping you embrace inferiority

I hugged mine like a long lost friend

yearning for apologies

in exchange for forgiveness

resolve came with forgiving myself

for taking the abuse

so I gave inferiority some dap

on the way out

I'm through

Peace.

Brotherly Love

I used to smile when he walked in the room. Knowing he was around was sufficient. Emulating his every movement from brushing his teeth to the way he scrambled his eggs. He had the faultlessness of a bishop and a name worth more than good credit. It was with him that I played my first arcade game and learned my first lesson in fighting my own battles. Zooming down the midnight streets that made the city lights look like stars embedded in brick galaxies. Tinted windows, a furry steering wheel and candy paint had the whole block looking at him the way I did. He later traded my company for the Caribbean sun and I buried my emotions in books and extracurricular activities. Seeing his face again turned my left and right brain into pro and con. We were two new people standing on an old street with old expectations and new experiences. We never came close to the interaction I valued in times past. I later learned that he hated me...simply because I'm his brother.

A Sister's Guidance

(To Aunty Flo)

She tells me it's not about the pain people give me

or the lack of concern for my feelings

can't control that

trying is futile

it's more about the me I give to people

in what kind of package

and how it's delivered

ideas ideals and ideologies

are fragile

handle with care

frustration only strengthens pain

finding laughter in life is an antibiotic

afford the luxury of gentleness she says

weakness is yet another thing

always tempted to ask her

why I should walk this way

cuz we always cry together

what's the point

wiping her eyes she says

crying makes laughter feel better

and I guess you live to gain the things

you use when you come back

like and elder earns the right

to sit in a rocking chair

and talk to the wind

LIFE'S

HIGHWAY

"A traveler am I and a navigator, and everyday I discover a new region in my soul. " – Kahlil Gibran

That Red Book

She seemed lost in a book with a bright red cover

that was her escape

from the hustle and bustle of 8 am rush hour

constantly juggling the book's captivation

and maintaining her standing balance

as the train swayed her between me

and the unknown person

slightly brushing her back with theirs

her eyes sliding across the page

like typewriters of antiquity

I bobbed my head to the beat in my headphones

and the groove the train made

as it traveled between stations

my eyes studying her brown coat

that matched her hair like a Dutch Boy sample

accenting her all black outfit

my mind became flooded with thoughts

of her hips bearing my child

those soft sculptured calves resting on my legs

as we watch tv

during a too cold to go out Sunday

her long brown hair tickling my cheek

and that damn red book

sitting on the table

way across the room.

Between St. Johns and Sterling

The only house

on the block

with a green door

walls with old Hebrew prayers hidden in the frame

a large family chasing more dreams

than a fat cat in the winter

Mama praying to the sunrise

thankful for another opportunity to kiss her children

Daddy squeezing us

to remind us of his adoration

and his strength

instructions

silver savings bonds redeemed for sweets

that accompanied our notebooks

and family pride

stepping out on faith in the streets

trying hard not to be of it

common sense was the rule

and ruler

but somehow we've missed a step

tripping up on the same values that preserved us

having green doors meant we were down to earth

but sometimes I wish they were blue

so we'd be as fluid as the sea

limitless as the sky

instead we're stuck

somewhere between St. Johns

and Sterling Place

Africa in Brooklyn

a village of brick buildings

each with distinct tribal noises

metal horses

parked alongside the pathway between dwelling place

and the road

children play outside

using the perfect mixture of imagination

and anything they can get their hands on

creating games

that pass the time

before the moon kisses the clouds goodnight

strong female hands

meld together

love and nutrition on plates

laden with family heritage

late night

the elders give praise to ancestors

with golden horns

string

goatskin

sharing parables of the lessons

only a lifetime could teach

 jobbers pass by

offering the latest

in creatively attained merchandise

an occasional war or two

over territory

woman

or reputation

followed by flowers

candles and liquor libation

but the world continues to turn

as a part of a universal wheel

the sun will rise yet again

and people move their feet

until the day is done

Africa

right here in Brooklyn

Global MLK

concrete connoisseurs

doing tricks for treats

donning layers of pieces

patches

to keep warm

reading faces for approach approval

very little shame

pride perpetuates hunger

strolling strips

'round corners

lurking unoccupied buildings

with wrinkles in their faces

a stone's throw from lavish lofts

trendy businesses

hustling for a high

trying to make heaven out of a hard time

brother can you spare a dime

long gone

it's the day of the dollar

inflation living lavish

right next door to suffering

and they both

have a million cousins

this is any hood

anywhere

everywhere

across the globe

there might even be one on Mars

you never know

Innocent Inquiries

His young mind

was filled with more questions

than his cute little hat could contain.

He asked her about his shoes,

the candy he kept dropping,

the bridge he saw

through the subway car window

and the arch in her eyebrows.

He also asked about me,

but my construction boots

and urban labels

made her afraid

of who she thought I might be.

So she looked down

and waited for a different question.

Ignorant Discomfort

typical morning

alarm clock

shower

deodorant

khakis

shoes

and jacket

slide out to catch the 8:05

get a bagel on the way

swipe your card

put a token in

skip down the stairs

push and shove to the multicolored benches

open a book

turn the headphones up

the train can be loud sometimes

a chunky sister

that's cooked more than her share of curry goat

akee

cod fish

and dumplings

decides to squeeze into a partial seat

calculations of size obviously in error

serving soliloquy of mass transit expenses

no tact

no respect of persons

undesirable attitude

and ignorance

change soulful elder

to bitch

turn the music louder

heads shaking in disgust

shit

and we ain't even leave Brooklyn yet

Just Like it Used to Be

She began looking at them

like the outcasts

looked at the in-crowd

across the junior high school lunchroom

her lips began to curl as if in utter disgust

she hated everything about them

I think it was the long hair

the perfect make up

and the we-are-going-somewhere-you're-not buzz of the conversation

that reminded her of her adolescent self-hate issues

they entered the train the same time I did

and I was too wrapped up in my new CD to bother

but she was attentive

as if to create more ammunition

for her ill feelings towards them

or rather the painful memory of people of their kind

her eyes were focused

as they peered

at these women

from under the brim of her large wool hat

as for them

they continued to talk

paying her no attention

just like in the 6th grade

it was written all over her face

she just had a head on collision with her youthful
insecurities

BEING SUPREME

"God is a circle whose diameter is everywhere and whose circumference is nowhere. " – Sufi Proverb

Dear GOD,

Thank you for being YOU and allowing me to be myself.
YOU understand when no one else does. Words are but a
formality when We speak cuz YOU do most of the talking.
I pray my actions validate my desire to be a good listener.
Nature serves as a postcard signed with your love and I've
written back to say thank you.

Love,

Me

P. S. Tell the angels I save their voicemails.

Interesting Thought

God is a woman

mysterious

understanding

a great listener

a soft breeze

when temperatures rise

loving hands

silent strength

God is a man

stern disciplinarian

protector

equalizer

God is everything

and nothing

cuz even that's something

Chosen and Thankful

it was the day I couldn't pay my rent and my bills in the
same week

counting hours to the Friday

I could buy myself a decent lunch

and it was only Wednesday

sifting through the change

to buy my favorite snack

hoping favoritism

would help to hush the evening hunger pains

wondering when I'd be able to take my clothes to the
cleaners

just to look better

than I was feeling

the old living room carpet

was a representation of the wish-I-could-change-the-
situation blues

staring at the wall

thinking the answer

would etch itself in the paint

it was the day I decided something had to be done

Poetry had chosen me

and I was going to thank her

Who's Gonna Go

Imagining heaven as my mother described its brilliance.

No pain or suffering,

love and peace for eternity.

But who's gonna go?

Is it the Christians who believe in Christ's redemption of our sins?

What about Mohammed,

Allah's messenger?

Is his message valid?

Does the name Yahweh hold any weight

or do the teachings of the Torah

drift in the wind as autumn leaves?

Are the 5 pillars but a waste of celestial material?

Is the Bible a holy synonym for Outkast's Art of Storytellin'?

And by the way, who's their master?

What about the televangelists

that steal the sticker on redemption marked

"No Purchase Necessary"?

Is life an open book test

with the hardest part being to choose the right book?

Or is it the one on the left?

Will my life be measured by my faults

or the fact that I admitted them?

Is the Yoruba religion witchcraft?

Or are people not ready for real West African culture?

I wonder how Zoraster would describe the idea of heaven?

Does the Spirit speak to the Chinese in Chinese?

Or does the ever-present language barrier exist?

Will white people go first like in chess

and Black folks picket around the pearly gates for 400
years?

I mean really, is hip hop music all that bad?

Or is it the truth folks are afraid of?

So tell me who's gonna go?

Amen Lights

Built like fortresses

around our lives

parked next to venues serving vices

advocating a heaven

higher than project roofs in the summer of '85

hoarding cheese

getting over like a fat rat

reciprocity rare like courteous cops

standing room sardine-packed with Jenkins

Johnsons

Robinsons

Williams

Wilsons

humming on time

to soliloquy from pastor

who learned from master

that receiving feels so much better than giving

vampires leaving hickies on community corners

just cuz the drug dealers left doesn't mean you're right

or even on point

powdered milk

and vegetarian beans

are a start

but we need a lifetime of nourishment

remember

Jesus fed the poor

'til they were filled

he didn't show up to the Mount

on the shiniest

bestest

horse

he walked

Church on Saturday

I go to church on Saturday

where I jook my joints to simulated hand claps

wiggle my ligaments to the scratchy voice of the turntables

hands are raised in affirmation of a sermon to the streets

no matter how fictitious

hearts strings plucked in harmony with hypnotizing
percussion arrangements

catching the spirit is as easy as donating to the building
fund

see in this church the dj acts as preacher

the bartenders collect the offering

and the ushers will show you the door

if the wine from communion has somehow gone to your
head

exotic hats

fancy jewelry

and high end clothing are still the standard

when the beat drops

adamant believers make their way to the front

dancing in the aisles is definitely permitted

As usual,

the service ends with announcement of next week's
gathering

and the benediction is to get home safe.

A Thought or Two or Three

it's nothing less than wonder

droplets racing each other to the cement

thunder closing in on its highly mobile counterpart

creative sector signaling the heart to drum

to the beat of small electric pulses

all in His hands

the breath of life

His to bestow upon us

inklings

in this vast universe

of beings

tangible and intangible

Simplicity, Complexity and Miracle sit at the same table of Understanding

Life, Love and Happiness two tables down

across from Wisdom and Experience

at a table for two

all in His house

Time ran out

she had to leave early

Knowledge moved from table to table

what you think of…

just watching rain

Thank God

sliding feet

waving hands

smiling to the beats played for the funk god

moving the way you feel

cuz living in and of itself is a task

minds freed from daily oppression

associated with our attraction for each other

and creating means for a prosperous lifestyle

enjoying the time we show the floor

what we've been through for the past week

appreciating the lead heavy air

for being a distraction to our personalized demons

baptized in the sea of our sweat

grooving to percussion

that speaks to our desire for liberation

each step

stomp

twist

reminding us of our power

to change the current situation

whatever that maybe

it's the way we use our carnal faculties

to express the deepest gratitude to the Creator

you may have a different way

this is ours

AND THE MORAL OF THE STORY IS...

"The chief obstacle to the progress of the human race is the human race. " – Don Marquis

A is for Africa…B is for Black

(In Memory of Pre-Educational Day School)

As a child,

my mind was tuned

for the reception of religion

as a part of my identity.

While others played,

I prayed.

Studied the Bible

and the ideals of a Being with no last name.

My mind stimulated

by the sound of a bell

surrounded by roses

and ladies with white head wraps and decorative aprons,

disciplined by the significance of incense, praises and
khufis

or mesmerized

by the hand clappin', foot stompin' Holy Ghost filled folk.

I can remember poetry

to the beat of a drum during Kwanzaa,

simulated celebrations of Canaan

and emulating the wisdom of three men who followed a star.

Life was irregular,

peculiar

and indoctrinating.

As I think back

it started with two phrases,

"A is for Africa…B is for Black."

The Day the Lights Went Out

My metrocard didn't work that day

wishing tokens hadn't gone out of style

no way to get around

water flip flops and fresh fruit

were the cash crops

cuz nothing was being sold on credit

all that walking

gave me time

to think about

the kid

that waited 20 min

to be declined his first Big Mac

the five second eternity

in a dark operating room

the chick he was supposed to meet

on West Fourth

at 8pm

the anxious college freshman

waiting to board the plane at LaGuardia

online romance going South

before winter

only hearing half of Naima

her wash and set

not drying all the way

an incomplete airbrush interpretation of a rock and roll
legend

an X Box

fresh out of the box

interrupted marriage proposal via cell phone

a reality check

a reminder

a cosmic public service announcement

just to let us know

the only things that really last

are love community and common sense

I guess Moms was right

Simple Enjoyment

amazed at how

we used to

share those twin sized beds

elated by the freedom to love

like those crazy tv sitcoms

nothing more to offer than a meal plan

a few goodies from Wal Mart

affection with little stipulation

save decent personal hygiene

if that

easy living

a series of guided routines

with spurts of excitement every now and then

highly anticipating life

on the other side of four years

thinking the grass is greener

it ain't

they just pay landscapers

to tender the lawn

closest to your side of the fence

enjoy the simple life

trust me

Colored People's Time

found out

why our shoes

make waves on the pavement

it's our sense of time

we ride

the same arc

as the Sun in July

slow flow on the curve of December

the moon our flashlight

as we admire

the stellar decoration

of the neighborhood outdoor den

getting there

is a few soul handshakes

and head nods away

greeting each other is our custom

especially before travel

clothes have to match emotion

or act as a balance

the mirror listens to our secret conversation

before journeying the battleground of daily living

with all its wiles

no matter how late

we arrive on time

to do what we must

make everything better

some of us just take it a little too far

Me & You

Unsure

of what I will do next

certain only

that I am determined to live longer

than other messengers

who discovered humanity is worth preserving

unscathed by surface scratching misconceptions

and nasty looks in Midtown

I notice myself in everyone

whose eyes meet mine

even those who don't

my aim

is to live with purpose like

Malcolm after Mecca

Ghandi after getting thrown of a train

Mama after Reagan

Jesus after Gethsemane

we all bleed red

when skin is pierced

release tear duct secretions

when in pain

cross our fingers

when in need of hope

 I am you

you are me

I am he

You

Someone Asked the Question

confused

I grab my pen, clutch it tight

finesse it

to create the scribblings

that liberate this haven of emotions, thoughts, prayers,
meditations, cares, worries.

I haven't quite mastered my tone,

cadences

or trademark topic.

I try to free my mind with each line

it doesn't always have to rhyme

or hit everyone in the room,

space

or continuum

at the same time

and

there are occasions when the message is sublime.

I scratch my head

to pause and scan the mental thesaurus

for the word, words and catch phrases

then it comes to me

the word,

line

or rhyme

to keep it on time

I pray

the Creator

continues

to enlighten

and the juices

keep flowin'

and

I

through Him

continue

writin'.

Just Sometimes

sometimes I wish I didn't need you

want you

crave your very essence

think you were required to sustain me

sometimes I wish I didn't pray that we'd be together

wanna play with your hair

or just lay there

watching you breathe deep

with your eyes closed

sometimes I wish I could move through this life

by myself

wanting nothing more

than basic needs

clean clothes

food in my stomach

and shoes on my feet

sometimes I wish all I needed was music

and summer solstice

no credit cards

or health insurance

sometimes I wish my family would leave me alone

deal with their own issues

and take weekly listening workshops

sometimes I wish people would be honest

about why they feel inferior

and stop being miserable

cuz they forgot how to fly

it's not how I feel all the time

just sometimes.

Maybe She Wanted to Talk

beckoning me to arise from my slumber

like a child before Saturday morning cartoons

she nudged me back to semi consciousness

not sure if it was the way she called my name

or the persistent steady press of her little fingers

but my eyes were opened

immobile

with little ability

I beheld her

seemingly shy

humble frame in a white scalloped blouse

plain black skirt

her face blurry

my body pleading with God

to escape this weird limbo between realities

my prayers answered

she disappeared

and a lifetime of fears relinquished

maybe she wanted to talk

a lesson in being still

and silent

Two Minutes Before Or Was it After

I had a dream last night

with drums and their rhythms

bouncing off the dialects of many o' cultured beings.

The barriers seemed to dissipate

in this room full of young souls –

all of which I had encountered

at one time or another in my life.

Confusion was kicked out

and Misunderstanding took notes

in this forum of togetherness.

My mind,

bewildered at first,

was enslaved by the aura

and enlightenment of the souls present.

There was one man in particular

with a natural crown on his head

and skin as rich as fertile soil.

He told us we could fly if we wanted to

and the realization of our dreams

were as serious as a marital vow.

His hands mimicked the movements of his words

to the canvas of our eardrums.

He spoke with conviction,

possibly possessed and

his words were a testimony to our spiritual nature.

He told us we could fly

and I believed him.

BEHIND

THE

MUSIC

"Music makes me forget, makes me remember." –
Deborah June Lockwood

B – Boys

'burban bad boys

breathe binary blurbs

bleaching beguiled babes

branding bitches

boasting bravado

between business bribes

bleeding black beginnings

bending brotherly bonds beneath betterment

bashing beauty beyond belief

bomb beats bewildered believers

building beefs boldly before bass

but Baghdad's bombs

bring back beforeness

blessed be backset blockers

b – boys

The DJs Request

Like a hot plate of home cooked helpings

they draw you to the table of movement

hoping your feet

disagree with your need to look cute

or cool

or just plain look

facilitating the marriage of intrinsic message

and extrinsic beat

designed with the intent of dragging you to center space

it's been a while since you've had an alignment

via swirling hips

and exaggerated shoulder shrugs

time to move from the comfort of the drink du jour

to the arena of human funk

and organized confusion

never know when a song will grab you

there's no telling where it will lead

Dance

it'll set you free

if you can't

nod your head

freedom will find you.

Lollygag

It's the way the wind sounds

between the reed and his fingers

via metal tubing

shaped like the pipeline to the prettiest girl's heart

it's a high

that makes you look at the lights in the ceiling

pulsate to the sweaty beat of hard-pressed skin

kissing tapered wood

or the low

that makes you look at the shine of your wingtips

and stretch across the chair

pressed against the darling at your table

it's a lollygag

a swagger

a tilt to the side

daddy-what-you-know jive

one time for your mind

troubled thoughts aside

it's a funky bop

groovy shoo wop tadow

it's Joe Henderson on tenor sax

Passing in the Night

Wes the idealist

playing a guitar that tiptoes the scales like tickling feathers

his fingers do *ntore* across smoothed out strings

just can't hear that

without thinking of the scent of aged grapes

and old oak

trickling down crystal stemware

after an extravagant entree

pinstripes belong here

it's the guy with the bulky silver tie kinda groove

fingers pop to the live bass drop

ditty bop

ba dop

feet lodged in spit shine modern day moccasins

tap on time

cherry red cigar ends like an infrared hip-to-the-game
signal

drowning in a person's love for music

the essence of conscious pass time

Southern Lakes on Saturn

the lovechild of Aganju's wanting for Yemonja

cuz the night he was born

the moon was a fiery red

feelings of being misunderstood

screamed between the guitar strings popping their neck

to the quick deliberate strum of ambidextrous ambition

he served in the military the same time he fell in love with
music

blessed with the opportunity to hear the sound barrier
broken

while testing machinery our tax dollars support

he vowed to share what he heard with the world

this is why he can make his five-stringed arm extension

sound interstellar

using comparative metaphors

to tell us about ourselves

via his perpetual love quest

it's like a conversation with autobiographical undertones

cloaked in riddle

in other words

you have to actually listen

he told us about the love that created him,

sustained him

and how love had taken him higher

slowing him down was not in the equation

stepping into his arena meant discarding a false sense of
stability

taking chances would be a mere pass time

the understanding of a higher consciousness the standard

he described the paradox of his existence

as being here

and simultaneously a million miles away

I agree

so come with me

we have many miles to go

The Game Don't Play

A Shakespearean tragedy set in Brooklyn

a hustler's tale of love

that made big dudes realize

our words are smooth enough

to pull chicks that didn't talk to us

at PS 167

the story of a woman that was cool

with a man really being himself

and would swiftly let him know

or rather

understand

that she is equally as ruthless

with enough mind power

to tame her natural moodiness

the quiet cutie from down the street

you had no idea smoked weed

cuz she was that low key

he came home one day

found her dead

as the drug game

is ironically

not about playing

he learned early

that crime pays back

nursing the wounds of loss

any way he could

it was music that helped us to remember

and forget

these days

we're trying to make hip hop

out of 50 cents

Untitled #120

Delighted by his choice of tunes

she nods to the same beat

he hears between the slide of the fader

there's something about a dj's selection

that teleports you to the planet where folks sit on rainbows

and sip ice tea

out of family size mayonnaise jars

after the storm

feet swinging in the wind

humming whatever you hear in your head

toying with the effect of the echo

between your voice and the jar

to the place where human secretion

offers libation to the fabric of your underclothes

as your feet move in appreciation

of how the music tickles your inner freedom

gliding across the floor

in ways you did in a previous life

wondering if there is a red clay district in the Motor City

or perhaps a Zone 3

the fader returns to its original position

Stevie lets you try on his glasses

seeing living things only by their aura

outward appearance tertiary to spiritual essence

and healing potential

listen closely

you'll hear Love harmonizing with the chords

she was the reverb of Jimi's guitar strings

they had lunch the summer before he crossed the Graffiti
Bridge

that's when he found out Love can't be tied down

cuz she's married to Revolution

MY

LIFE

AFTER

DEATH

"Death ain't the shit, but it's pleasant…kinda quiet…" – Christopher Wallace

When the Time Comes

And if I should pass before you think it was my time to go

don't cry

smile

and know that I've served my purpose in the material plane

Think of all the times we've laughed

and you shook your head

in pure disbelief of my crazy acts

Or our decisions on music and how we couldn't wait for that new CD to hit the stores

only to find out that half the time we traded it in for another one

Or the days Mother Nature couldn't even stop us from playing handball

What about those days you comforted me through all the women I wish I could understand

You remember, maybe even better than I, the first time you heard my name

and how you wondered where in the world I came from

We can't go on without talking about our first parties

together

Didn't know a big brother could break it down like that,
did you?

What about the weekends and the looks we got

because we were the loudest people in the restaurant

Our first formal events, first loves and first dates

The days when you couldn't pay me to hit a jump shot

but I can sure finger roll

Your encouragement in my passion for music

Do you remember coming back after breaks from college

and acting as if we hadn't seen each other in years?

It sure felt like it though

Wipe those tears

and know

that your thoughts and memories

make me immortal.

Making Room

She was a mother to us all

bracelets harmonizing with clanking kitchen utensils

vigorously searching for the spoon

to mix iced tea

you swore only Celie knew how to make

it was like her cheek would kiss you when you greeted her

after you journeyed the slanted driveway

and into her home

her almond eyes dismantled all your defense mechanisms

she knew what was wrong

even if we didn't

she was as cool as a fan

as she seemingly floated around the kitchen

lodged between the room occupied with the sound of the sports channel

and the one where people never sat on the couch

she lived in Middle America

where even the hood had trees

big ones

as big as her heart

she was a blessing to everyone that wiped their feet on the rug outside her door

but she got tired and decided to move out

to make room for another one

another blessing

Around the Block and Back

She was around when cabarets really consisted of live entertainment.

If a person pulled a gun,

it was a big deal.

Somebody really made a player mad.

Back then only about four cars could fit on a city block

and every brother had a signature hat.

She was around when you really had to know how to sing

to make a record,

people actually learned something in school,

kids ate at the table

and your parents wanted to see Soul Train as much as you did.

She was around when Christmas was really about giving,

seeing people's faces light up when they got Gramma's famous envelope.

I can't remember a year I didn't look forward to that

and the only thing she wanted in return was a dance when
the music started.

She was around when Brooklyn streets weren't named
after Black folks,

when the new church used to be a theatre,

when you could order a triple fudge sundae at a diner,

when Black folks knew the time.

She was around.

In our lives just to show us

that you live,

you love,

you learn

and you leave

to live on

in someone's fondest memory.

To Dani

She had the ability to look right through me.

Her eyes

were the windows

to understanding how difficult it is

to be young, attractive and intelligent.

She was one of Love's children,

an example

of what it is to go through life

and still enjoy the simple beauty of a flower

in an unexpected location.

She told the truth

and the rest was just none of your business.

She moved you

without trying to appear deep

or impudent.

She was wonderful.

She just wanted to find warmth in a cold world.

And she did...

just not here.

To Junior

Someone was blown away

and his mind wasn't the only thing that left

His body lay like a brick in the ocean.

Callin' 911 proved that we're still 3/5 a man

and there is truly no love in the heart of the city.

Cops moving slow enough

to make you wonder

if they wanted him to die on the pavement.

Askin' who dunnit questions

like we forgot they hate us.

Well I didn't see shit,

all I heard was screamin from the window.

I ran outside only to see people crowded around a
wounded soul

as usual the women were crying

and street smart associates ended every sentence with son.

They said the gunshots were loud

but not as loud as the mother of his child

when she found out his spirit

evacuated his now lifeless shell.

Another soldier down,

another fatherless child,

another two weeks of candles

on the last spot we saw him smile.

To Gene

Not bad

just misguided

he played handball to pass the time

hustled so time wouldn't take the lead

the bounce in his walk matched the sidewinding hook of the ball

leaving no room for mistaken identity

thought street life was romantic

though concrete doesn't give

it takes away

he knew better

not like that makes a difference

wrong doing is way more enticing

walk around

with the story of his mother

skipping town on the silver bullet

hoping he wouldn't have to take the same train

she hopped on years earlier

but we all know about fallen apples

and their distance from the tree

history has a way of repeating itself

with a twist

but at least they're together now

a son can only survive but so long

without his mother

The Day Shazzam Died

I bet he was in high school

when this cartoon

was a part of our regularly scheduled programming

the lightning bolt super hero

Hanna Barbera's version of Shango

I guess that's why he liked him

he was what your grandmother would call strapping

healthy

his arms like ten inch thick lead pipes

swaying inversely with his feet

yeah he was strong

but it was his faster-than-the-speed-of-sound smile

that made him amazing

On one of these cool Saturday evenings

he tried to save someone's life

and prevent them from breaking the law

he told them not to smoke

in a not-so-ventilated bar

on Manhattan's Lower East Side

and they killed him

just for being the neighborhood super hero

and I know that they aren't supposed to die

super heroes I mean

but that was the day Shazzam died

Alvin is Dead

Alvin

young and optimistic

passive

no opinion

no argument

no rebuttal, verbal attack or harsh remark

no problem

servant to all

warm hands and an even warmer heart

blind love

unconditional

no grudges

well not for long anyway

a strong belief in the good that abides in all men

sensitive to human need

a giver when all you do is take

accommodating

liked by all

no reproach

no stance

no pro

no con

no defense mechanisms

just open

no anger

no malice

just honesty and humility

no reaction

no more

'cause Alvin is dead,

dead and gone.

the eulogy I wrote while living

I walk to the beat of a god

that learned how to drum

from the most unorthodox player in the village

overcome fear

like the way white folks

look at Black babies sit next to them on the train

I spend a lot of time there

on the train

I know what crack is like

cuz I roam the streets at night

looking for someone who'd sell me a pen

writing words about phrases

that tell stories of love and Zen

and then

channel bop tunes

through the strands of my hair

synthesize to synchronized movements of tone and air

live like a rich kid

wondering only what dream I can achieve next

look at lives past

learning a part of the half

by perusing some text

eat to fuel my feet

as they groove on tiled basements

pull asunder all but thunder

to touch lives and talk about the basics

I've learned to fly

via my imagination

just to leave the block

found a match

that doesn't go outta style

like black dress socks

take people to a world

seen only when I'm by myself

so don't cry for me

I lived wonderfully

and just living is having wealth

ABOUT THE AUTHOR

Sugar Johnson (Ugarhon Serrette) hails from the Crown Heights section of Brooklyn with a brief stint in the Caribbean during his formative years. After earning his B.A. in Mathematics from DePauw University, Johnson worked as an analyst in the corporate sector before teaching poetry in the New York City Public School system. The burgeoning writer, actor and vocalist has shared the stage with prolific artists such as Bob Holman, Jessica Care Moore, Spike Lee, Robert Galinsky and Ursula Rucker...just to name a few. Johnson currently lives in Atlanta where he continues laboring for students and steals an occasional moment or two on stage. He can be reached at sugarjbk@gmail.com